THE
SELVAGE

THE
SELVAGE

POEMS

LINDA GREGERSON

Houghton Mifflin Harcourt

Boston   New York   2012

For information about permission to reproduce selections from this book,
write to Permissions, Houghton Mifflin Harcourt Publishing Company,
215 Park Avenue South, New York, New York 10003.

www.hmhbooks.com

Library of Congress Cataloging-in-Publication Data
Gregerson, Linda.
The selvage : poems / Linda Gregerson.
p. cm.
ISBN 978-0-547-75009-5
I. Title.
PS3557.R425S45 2012
811'.54—dc23   2012015517

Book design by Greta D. Sibley

Printed in the United States of America
DOC 10 9 8 7 6 5 4 3 2 1

ACKNOWLEDGMENTS

The Atlantic Monthly: "Slight Tremor," "Constitutional," "Lately, I've taken to," "Varenna," "The Expulsion" (as "Saint Peter Released from Prison"), "The Baptism of the Neophytes"

The Boston Review: "Blink"

Granta: "Ariadne in Triumph"

The Kenyon Review: "Dido Refuses to Speak"

New England Review: "Theseus Forgetting"

The New Yorker: "Still Life"

Northwest Review: "His Shadow"

The Paris Review: "Slaters' Measure"

PN Review (UK): ". . . More Instructive Than a Long Trip to Europe," "Ovid in Exile," "Her Argument for the Existence of God"

Poetry: "The Selvage," "Pajama Quotient"

Poetry Review (UK): "The Death of Ananias," "The Tribute Money"

TriQuarterly: "Catch"

"Dido Refuses to Speak" was reprinted in *The Pushcart Prize XXXV* (2010).

"The Selvage" was reprinted in *Cork Literary Review* (Ireland, 2011), in *The Alhambra Poetry Calendar 2012*, ed. Shafiq Naz, and in *Saying What Happened: American Poetry after the Millennium*, ed. Ann Keniston and Jeffrey Gray (McFarland, 2012). "Still Life" was also reprinted in *Saying What Happened.*

"Getting and Spending" was commissioned by the Folger Shakespeare Library to accompany an exhibition of writing by early modern women. It was first published in *Shakespeare's Sisters: Women Writers Bridge Five Centuries,* ed. Gigi Bradford and Louisa Newlin (Folger Shakespeare Library, 2012).

My thanks to the Rockefeller Foundation and the Liguria Study Center for residencies at Bellagio and Bogliasco, where a number of these poems were written, and to the University of Michigan and the College of Literature, Science, and the Arts for continuing support.

And to David Baker and Michael Collier, best of counselors.

CONTENTS

Steven

No gate, but like one

—*Edmund Spenser*, The Faerie Queene, *II.xii.53*

THE
SELVAGE

THE SELVAGE

So door to door among the shotgun
shacks in Cullowhee and Waynesville in
our cleanest shirts and *ma'am*
and *excuse me* were all but second

nature now and this one woman comes
to the door she must have weighed
three hundred pounds Would you be
willing to tell us who you plan to vote

for we say and she turns around with
Everett who're we voting for? The
black guy says Everett. The black guy
she says except that wasn't the language

they used they used the word
we've all agreed to banish from even our
innermost thoughts, which is when
I knew he was going to win.

2

At which point the speaker discovers,
as if the lesson were new,
she has told the story at her own expense.
Amazing, said my sister's chairman's

second wife, to think what you've
amounted to considering where you're from,
which she imagined was a compliment.
One country, friends. Where when

we have to go there, as, depend
upon it, fat or thin, regenerate
or blinkered-to-the-end, we shall,
they have to take us in. I saw

3

a riverful of geese as I drove home across
our one-lane bridge. Four hundred of them
easily, close-massed against the current and
the bitter wind (some settled on the ice) and just

the few at a time who'd loosen rank to
gather again downstream. As if
to paraphrase. The fabric
every minute bound

by just that pulling-out that holds
the raveling together. You were driving
all this time? said Steven. Counting
geese? (The snow falling into the river.)

No. (The river about
to give itself over to ice.) I'd stopped.
Their wingspans, had they not
been taking shelter here, as wide as we are tall.

Pajama Quotient

Coinage of the not-yet-wholly-
      hardened custodians of public
health, as health is roughly measured
      in the rougher parts of Dearborn.

Meaning, how many parents,
      when things get bad, are wearing
what they've slept in when they come
      to pick up the kids at school.

The best of talk, said someone
      once, is shop talk: we can go
to it as to a well. But manifolds
      and steering racks are going

the way of the wells—offshore—
      so the-nifty-thing-you-do-
with-the-wrench-when-the-foreman-
      has-sped-the-line-up

has become a ghastly shorthand for
      despair among the people
you are paid to help. Despair,
      sometimes, of helping. In

the winter dawn a decade and a half
        ago, we'd gather around
the schoolbus stop—the unshaved
        fathers, mothers, dogs,

the siblings in their snowsuits—so
        the children bound for
Johnson Elementary might have
        a proper sending-off.

The privileged of the earth, in our
        case: words and stars
and molecules were all our care,
        a makeshift village blessed

with time and purpose. And
        a schoolbus stop,
to make it seem like life. By far my
        favorites were the Russian

mathematicians: bathrobes hanging
        below their parkas, cigarettes
scattering ash, their little ones for the
        moment quite forgotten, they

would cover the walls of the shelter
        with what

to most of us was Greek but was
  no doubt of urgent consequence

for quantum fields. So filled with joy:
  their permanent markers on the
brick. And then
  the bus, and then the children off

without us and our little human pretext
  gone. Fragile the minutes.
Fragile the line between wonder
  and woe. The poet when he

wrote about our parents in the garden
  gave them love and rest
and mindfulness. But first
  he gave them honest work.

SLIGHT TREMOR

The fine fourth finger
of his fine right hand,

just slightly, when
he's tracking our path

on his iPhone or
repairing the clasp

on my watch I
will not think about

the myelin sheath.
Slight tremor only,

transient, so
the flaw in the

pavement must
have been my

mother's back.

Constitutional

O. G., 1872–1962

It's a wonder they didn't all of them die of the
        sun those days. Remember
Ole's forehead and the backs of his hands?
The fair-haired sons of Norway in their bright
        Wisconsin fields, the map

of blessed second chances writ in tasseled
        corn. (The damage writ
in melanin.) I never could stand it, my father
would say, by which he meant the morning
        constitutional: the dose

of electric fencing Ole found was just the
        cure for frozen joints.
But joints be damned, the rest of it my father
loved, he'd cast about for a portion I
        could manage, maybe

    Linda could fetch the cows. Poor man. He little
        thought how quickly
the race declines. *Ourselves and our posterity.*
It all alarmed me: dung slicks, culvert, swollen
        teats, the single narrow

wire above the barbed ones, commotion
        of flies on the rim
of the pail. We're better at living on paper,
some of us, better at blessings already
        secured. The fence?

It was for animals. And insulated, quaintly,
        with a species of porcelain
knob. That part, at least, I had the wit
to find benign, like the basket of straw-flecked
        eggs. A touch of homely

caution in the liable-to-turn-on-us world.
        Ordain and establish.
And breakable too. An old man at his battery-
charged devotions, double-fisted on
        the six-volt fence. *In order*

to form. A measure of guesswork, a measure
        of faithful refraining-from-
harm, let us honor the virtues of form.
And all the dead in company, if only
        not to shame them.

SLATERS' MEASURE

SWEPT VALLEY

Which sounds like something the wind
    would do:
        acres of timothy bending

      beneath its touch, swift clouds,
their shadows running wanton
        on the sloping fields. But this

      is human-built, in stone.
    Where pitch of the roof meets
pitch of gabled dormer and, their

courses laid in twos
      and threes, the tapered slates
        describe a curving channel, there

      the rain may rain, the wind
may blow, the people beneath
        will still be warm. The beauty

      both a by-blow and a
    premise, as
in all the arts of usefulness.

Beneath which the quarryman
   crawls. Or rather
      shimmies on his side

   by lamplight, right
arm free to wield the single-bladed
      pick (no room

      for a backswing). Columns
   of ragstone left to support
the ceiling which, when near collapse,

emits a telltale series of clicks,
     the quarryman then retreating but
      no faster than

   the knocking down of columns
will allow. The broken ceiling,
      hauled in barrows to the

     surface, they call
  Collyweston slate. The clicks?
That part they call *talking*.

FROST

Because it isn't proper slate at all
            but limestone laced
                        with *quarry sap*, which

            is to say, with water, it
can only be split as the weather agrees
                        to help. Hard frost.

                        At which point, setting
            the *log* or block of stone on
edge, the miner taps the fault lines with

his hammer. When
            the winter stays ruthlessly mild, as is
                        so often, of late,

            the case, the stone
must be buried again in trenches lest the
                        water leach forever

                        away. Which means
            in turn the dressing months must go
to waste. An empty-handed June.

JURASSIC

When all the world above what we
                would later call the Midlands was
                                a shallow sea.

                And clean-
washed grains of what had been the
                                shells and bony body parts of

                                seaborne creatures settled
                on the saline floor.
Precipitants in the pore space, "like

the limescale in your kettle," and
                some hundred-and-sixty or sixty-
                                five million

                years. For this confusion (oolitic
as a structure versus
                                Lower Oolitic time)

                geologists admit
                some blame. For keeping off
the water use what water made.

SLATERS' MEASURE

Three to the case. Forty cases
    to the hundred. Seven hundreds
        to the heap, plus thirteen

    large, and all of them dressed.
Where wooden pegs
        will fasten the slate to the

        batting they use bill
    and helve to bore the hole.
Six shillings eightpence per annum per pit

(the slaters of course don't own the land)
    with an extra
        shilling and sixpence to the

    measurer. The rents
conveyed at an annual feast. When
        frosts have failed and night

        after night the stone must be
    watered, no wages at all. Who
pays for the feast my sources do not tell me.

CLEAVE

The rock, like the word, a paradox:
        where most it holds
                together (cleave) there also

        it's liable to split apart.
When did you first go down in the mines?
                I was fourteen, I hated

                the dark. *And school?*
        The slaters were my school. *And now
it's over?* Nearly over. I told you

about the frosts. Besides (there's no one
        speaking now) it's cheaper
                to salvage, you find

        some house that's falling down.
For gaps, they'd use a mossing
                iron, it forces

                the root mass in. So first
        a seabed then a garden and
the making a living in between.

WHEN THE ROMANS ARRIVED

with their trunk roads and their drainage
        schemes, they also
                imported the molding

        of red clay tiles.
But were alert
                to local idiom. So true

                slate in Carmarthenshire
        and Collyweston over here.
No tunneling yet, the outcrops still

sufficed, but they complained
        about the weather. These
                were hardship postings,

        ends of the earth.
And earth so long outlasts our little
                habitation—cleft

                in the rockface, fallen
        roof—our only natural
rhythm (it's a learned one) is the counterpoint.

Catch

You'd swear it was all
      improvisation—
mismatched piping, flatbed
      truck (its ancient

wheelbase straddling the bike
      lane), sacks (some
canvas discards from the Royal
      Mail) of elbow joints

and T-joints, and the three
      of them in hard hats
fitting shallow exoskeleton to
      brickwork (red

Victorian) with its cornices
      and bays—but you'd
be wrong, the rhythm's practiced,
      they have simply

favored function over show.
      Unless you count
the showy competence: the
      young one, on his

shoulder a stack of eight-foot
          planks, ascends
the ladder (right hand as a
          counterweight) and

(burden as lithe as the bearer)
          safely shelves what
might as easily have maimed
          a dozen passers-by on

               brackets where only this morning
          was only air. His friend
the foreman slides
          a double-story vertical,

two-handed, in its metal cuff
          (how useless two
on two will be if ever the
          piping starts to over-

balance) and, with one hand
          freed (the pipe extending
eighteen feet above him), pulls
          a socket wrench

and bolts the skybound strut
        in place. Some casual
treatment of potted plants (the
        neighbors having failed

to clear their balconies). Some
        whistling to the
partner on the ground. Then
        twice: the pliers

lofted, purest vertical, to
        tree height, work
height, slowing, nearly
        caught but by an inch

or two elusive, wonderfully
        sparing the casement
windows on their way back
        down. Again.

(By now the labor saved
        has long gone
theoretical.) (And none of it
        touching the labor the

scaffold itself is meant to serve.
            Re-grouting? Freshening
paint?) No matter. Once again.
            And so the rise, the

reach, the capture: bright
            alignment, like the heron
in its dive. The very pavements
            catch the gleam.

LATELY, I'VE TAKEN TO

guessing a lot,
             chiefly in
the auditory realm, where I
        am less and less

acute, which leads to masses
                of amusement
on the home front—Mom
            in orbit!—and what must

by now approximate
                a twenty-point
drop in the quotient we call
        IQ.

Endearing's not my
                strong suit
but I'll take what I can get.
        Forty percent

is what I thought I heard
                tonight but
surely that's not possible. All
        that ozone lost?

A single Arctic winter? I
                    had thought
those were the healing months
            for snowpack, but it

seems the stratospheric ice
                    does something
with the sunlight that's inim-
            ical. Unfriendly

in the long run to the cold.
                    So cold
against itself. Which we
            have done. Which, if

I may compare great things to
                    small, is what
my doctor thinks may be
            the trouble with my ear:

by-blow of the larger,
                    chronic
proneness to construe what might
            have been benign

as something to be fought.
              So malleus,
stapes, hammer and tongs. I've
              seen the enemy and he . . .

etc. On an island in
              the Tyrifjord
in Norway several days ago,
              a man who said

he'd come for their protection
              and, what's
worse, who with a not-before-un-
              heard-of-in-the-history-

of-the-world excuse for
              logic really
thought that was the case,
              hunted down and shot

as many people as he could.
              Obsession
at the barricades, which when
              it goes wrong in the body

we label as autoimmune.
                The body ingenious.
Body so resilient he
      chose hollow-point bullets

to better his odds. At least,
             said the girl in the
newscast, he was one
      of us, and everyone knew

exactly what she meant.

GETTING AND SPENDING

Isabella Whitney, "The maner of her Wyll"

I

We're told it was mostly the soul
    at stake, its formal

    setting-forth, as over water,
where, against all odds,

the words-on-paper make
    a sort of currency, which heaven,

    against all odds, accepts.
So *Will,* which is to say, May what

I purpose, please, this once, and what
    will happen coincide.

    To which the worldly
dispositions were mere afterthought:

your mother's ring and so forth. What
    the law considered yours

    to give. Which in the case of
women was restricted—this was

long ago, and elsewhere—so
        that one confessedly "weak

        of purse" might all the more
emphatically be thought of as having little

to say. Except about the soul. The late
        disturbance in religion

        having done that much, the each
for each responsible, even a servant,

even the poor. Wild, then—quite
        beyond the pale—to hustle

        the soul-part so hastily off
the page. And turn, our Isabella Whitney,

to the city and its faithlessness. Whose
        smells and sounds—the hawker's cry,

        the drainage ditch in Smithfield—all
the thick-laid, lovely, in-your-face-and-nostrils stuff

of getting-by no woman of even the slightest
        affectation would profess to know,

much less to know so well.
As one would know the special places on

his body, were the passion merely personal.

2

Wattle and brickwork. Marble and mud.
        The city's vast tautology. No city

    without people and no people but
will long for what the city says they lack:

high ceilings, gloves and laces, news,
        the hearth-lit circle of friendship, space

    for solitude, enough to eat.
And something like a foothold in the whole-of-it,

some without-which-not, some
        little but needful part in all the passing-

    from-hand-to-hand of it, so
every time the bondsman racks his debtor or

the shoemaker hammers a nail or one un-
        practiced girl imagines she

has prompted a look of wistfulness,
a piece of it is yours because

your seeing it has made it that much slower
to rejoin the blank

oblivion of never-having-
been. The year was fifteen hundred seventy-

three. The year of our Redeemer, as
they used to say. That other

circuit of always-in-your-
debt. From which she wrested, in her open

I-am-writing-not-for-fun-but-for-the-money
way of authorship, a world

not just of plenty but—and here's
the part that's legacy—of love.

ARIADNE IN TRIUMPH

Roman sarcophagus, second century CE

The stories are full of these women — Ariadne's
    only one — who cut all ties
to origin and nurture, to the very stones

    and grasses that have heretofore
spelled *home* and we are meant to understand
    they cannot help themselves: it's

love, their great addiction. The hero
    has other axes to grind.
Or clews to follow, something about the larger

    view, requiring
that he sacrifice the merely private sweetness
    of entanglement. To

which — the larger view — we leave him.
    Ariadne, meanwhile, though
abandoned, does better than most. See her here

    riding in triumph with
the god she's got as compensation. Ariadne
    at his back, her arm

and leg akimbo, one would never know
        she'd once been brought
so low. It's all before her now:

        the centaurs with their pipes
and lyre, the maenad mid-propulsion with
        her drum. The noise,

the dance, the will-there-be-sex-after-death
        of it, and Ariadne quite
unmoved. I think she likes the lioness.

        Who, striding
one way, gazes back and, just above her
        shoulder, sees exactly

what she's worth to all these revelers:
        an empty skin
that's worn by way of boasting See

        my prowess, as
her own six swollen teats proclaim
        Behold my fruitfulness.

No cubs in sight. As Ariadne has no
        children, just
the starry crown, which is a cleaner

sort of lastingness.
The better to capture what they must
    have hoped for who

commissioned the sculptor who chiseled
    the stone designed
to hold the body. When I came

    to the museum for a closer
look, the coffin was angled away from
    the wall: New plinth,

explained the carpenter, and let me see
    inside. Where I
beheld the warmer face of it. The

    stained, unfinished, pock-
marked face of breathable oblivion.
    My good wise friend

who does this for a living—makes
    the body's last lodging his daily
work—has no patience for

    the precepts of provident
use: my smallest portion of earth
    and so forth. Give

the dead their due, he says.
        With which
I'm loath to argue, but

        consider the plaque
on the wall: when Rome
        had not yet given up

her flawed republic, even the rich
        expected to come
to ash. The turn

        to empire favored
marble tombs. And also, as we've seen,
        required some respite

from the weight of all that
        permanence. Hence
Bacchic celebration, hence

        the woman's
mood. She'd give it all up in a heartbeat
        —that's the point

here—for the one
        whose lapse in memory
she's become.

THESEUS FORGETTING

It's all a sort of labyrinth:
    the way back out occluded while

        the monster the place was designed to contain
        still rages at its core. These aren't

the best of times for honor-under-pressure.
    And the girl, having foolishly fallen in love

        with a man her island had cause
        to hate, was no doubt ill advised

to fall asleep at all. So Theseus
    "forgot her." Or the teller of tales forgot

        to provide a motive for his hero, which
        has spawned a clutch of patchings-up,

not one of them not lame.
    What comes to us in pieces—think

        of Sappho on the midden heap—lays claim
        to us in ways the merely

perfect can't. And then
        when the story resumes, our man forgets

        again, this time the matter of changing
            the sails. Too plausible:

his head so full of triumphs and the shore
        so near . . . Which means his father,

        beholding the black-draped masts, believes
            his son has died and leaps,

despairing, from the cliff. Which means
        that Theseus is king.

        Were this another sort of story, we'd
            begin to sense a moral here:

ambition and its discards, for example. But
        the units of comprehension somehow

        aren't the ones we're used to, there's
            a piece gone missing, outsourced,

like causality, to petty gods. Does Theseus
        live to be sorry? Of course. And, as

it was the wisdom of the Greeks to see,
    for things quite unrelated.

Do you wish to be spared the sight
    of your children against the rocks?

You'd better time your dying right.

Dido Refuses to Speak

The forestays, the sternsheet,
        the benches,
   the yard,

        the wooden pins to which
   the oars are
bound with strips of leather, he

   explained this, thole
and loom, I thought the words
        were just as lovely as the

workings. And I thought
        I knew the principle:
   the moving forward facing where you've

        been, the muscled
   quarrel with the muscled sea, like
love, that sweet againstness. And

the linen sail:
happy the weaver whose work might bedeck
the chamber where we

lay us down. How strange
it seems from just a little distance:
the living tree, the ax,

the chisel, cattle
whom we kill and
skin, all so that they may live again on

water but including us.

2

Because she'd never not
                been there, my Anna (I
        can feel her now, the back

                of her hand as I hold it against
        my eyelid, I have always loved
to touch with eyes), because

        her voice was all the traction I'd ever
required, because
                so long as earth contained

precisely
                that measure of temple to eyebrow,
        eyebrow to lip, I knew

                I had a home, it was
        my sister I made
to make the thing ready—the firewood in

        its lofty escarpment, the torches,
the oil—and she, of course,
                when she asked what I meant to do,

to whom I lied. I meant
            my bitter heart to foul
        the wind that filled his sails. I did not ask

            what
        if the wind should change direction,
who would choke.

3

As when in early summer in the fields
                of silver thyme, the bees
        are thick with happy industry . . .

                As when the workmen trust
            their overseer to be just . . .
As when the world was tuned to us and we

        the world, my city
on its quarried footing rose and rang with
                purpose and

the water loved its channels and the
                terraces their civic flight
        of stairs. Reluctant

            evening, loath
        to lose the sight of them, would finger
the vertical facings until they

        blushed. I know
a better mind would not require
            the elements

to be like us, we smear

        our sorry longings on
the rocks and trees, but then

        the very daylight
seemed to say we'd built to scale.

4

Once in a narrow garden I
             encountered a thing I'd known
        before. A scent. I had

             no words for it. Not citron,
        though it bore that solvent
aptitude. Not anise, though it harbored

        a touch of clay. A fragrance I
had known as in another life,
             or this life, but before

the daily watering down. Which left me
             half transported on an un-
        distinguished plot of ground. So think

             what it meant when he began to
        speak. The story we'd stowed
as ballast on the fleeing ships, had painted

        on our temple walls, the very lights
and darks we had depended on to make
             the place less strange, and on

a stranger's lips. To whom
                    the story properly belonged. Or he
            to it, is there a difference? And

                    poor Dido mere excursus for them both.

5

If I burn the oars he won't be able to use them
to leave if I
lock up the winds in my cellar

if I shred the rigging or just
that pair of tendons at his inner
thigh not

so he suffers no but so he isn't able to
walk without help
and as for the eyes

he's already seen how I love him what need
for the eyes I was
—wasn't I?—young when the

other one came to me dressed
in his wounds which
wounds my brother gave him I

have ever . . . in faithfulness since but
mistaken the . . . yes or lost
the thread and now

these swarming . . . whom I
              welcomed as more of our own as
         on a carcass their indecent haste

              their blackened . . . when I ought . . .
         the tar-slicked hulls . . . And now
these trails of filthy mucus in the sand.

6

The child.
        I might
except for the child have been

        content.
But he in all his careless beauty—
cheekbone still untrammeled and the tidemark

        of hair at his nape—he sat
beside me where we ate,
        he laughed, his every un-

selfconscious bit of lassitude or
        fervor was
        a manifest that pled the father's case.

        There is no
outside to such arguments.
And surely I took precautions? What

        was true for me ought doubly to
have been the case for one whose
        future he

secured. So hostage both.

           All three. And now
I'm told he wasn't a

           child at all but a
god in the shape of a child.
Redundant.

7

Wasn't it nearly too sweet to be borne,
   that motherwit
  bought me a kingdom. *Every inch*

   that will fit in the oxhide.
  Which I shaved so fine,
in strips of such exquisite near-

  transparency, we thought the whole
of Africa might fall within our
   grasp. So dredged

the ports and felled the woodlands in the
   heady tide
  of heaven's bright approval . . .

   I am glad to find
  they haven't cut the woodland here.
Give me a margin of shadow, I'll tell you

  no lies. The myrtle
suits me, understory to
   the last, and mutes those sounds of

sorrow from the river. Not a single
                pine, no
        striving toward the masthead or the

        roofbeam, just
        these little purple blossoms, which
I do not take ironically.

        And best: the plates of silver
bark, which must be
                what happens to words.

From the Life of Saint Peter

Brancacci Chapel, Florence

I. HIS SHADOW

They brought us out on the pavement then,
our pallets
and cots, the
poorest barely decent in their bedclothes.
And facing

as best we could the sun,
so whether
he would or no his passing shadow might
pass over us and we
be healed. As if

some ghastly catalogue of everything you
fear the flesh
might one day have in store for you should
suddenly block
your way back home.

But look
how the painter has lovingly rendered the clubs
of my knees. Gall-
knots, hooves
of callus you would surely look away from in the

ordinary
course of things, calves
like an afterthought trailing behind. I wonder
will I get to keep some sign of this when I'm made
whole.

I've come to think
the body scorns hypothesis, hasn't it
paid for its losses
in kind? While we are writ in water. My
advantage here

was learning so early how little the world will
spare us. Now
this rumored cure:
You see
the peeling fresco? It was once as chaste as you.

2. THE DEATH OF ANANIAS

There must have been something with-
               held as if
you know the story you'll
      know has been said about me.

I saw what we all saw: goats and cattle,
               grain,
one ancient and three newer family
      houses and finally

the second-best vineyard for miles around
               converted
into silver and simply
      laid on the ground at their feet.

And namely the one called Peter: how
               is it
that one among equals will seem
      to have harnessed the moon

and stars. I understood the next
               part, how the
logic went: we hadn't been
      savages all our lives, we'd helped

the poor before. But this was something
                        else, was like
the dizzying vista above the gorge:
               you think you've been quite

happy, your loved ones are waiting to
                      welcome you
home and you can taste the broken rocks
              below through all your broken

teeth, you know the terror won't be
                       over until
you've thrown your one allotted life
              away. And so

I stepped back, just a little, from the
                       edge.
What kind of reckoning after all requires
              this all-or-nothing? Hadn't I

torn the lovely acres from my heart?
                       Which he
esteemed as so much filth. The least
              that would keep the cold off, that's

all I'd intended to put aside. You
                       see?
And cold came up to seize me.

3. THE TRIBUTE MONEY

Then, said my Master, *are the children*
          free. Which you might think
                    would tell us what to do

          but we had caught the scent
of parable. So hook, so fish, the
                    money in its mouth,

                    the mucus and blood
          on the money. I paid the collector
as I'd been told and part

was the lesson and part was speaking
          truth to power and still
                    there's part left over.

          From whom, he said, do the kings
of the earth extract their tribute?
                    Shining in its mouth as

          shines the golden hair
          you see to my left in the picture. From
the stranger, we said. But he

59

my Master loved said nothing, nothing
        but beauty was ever required
            of him. *Then are*

       the children free. Now look,
I'm not immune to this, I like
            to work the likeness out:

           for *pieces of money* read
     gifts of the earth, for *hook*
read *yours for the asking.* But as to

the one with golden hair, read what?
        That some shall leap while others
           crawl? That even

       the best of love is partial?
The fish that flashed a thousand
           colors, though you throw

       him back, will drown.
Which makes me think
the gills in their air-scorched frenzy must

extract some tribute too.

4. THE EXPULSION

*with: The Earthly Paradise, Saint Peter
in Prison, Saint Peter Released*

So whether you read from left
    to right (sent howling

    from the garden where
the stories all begin) or simply

wander as gaps in the crowd
    permit, the pillars of the

    chapel will have told you
how to navigate. On one side

the pair of them driven like
    cattle, her face with its

    sockets of grief. And on
the other side the premise still

unspoilt. Or is it promise? Where
    the sword and angel

    haven't yet obscured
the sky. You're thinking it's all

been lost on me, you've smiled
     to find me sleeping while

     the prisoner goes free.
But some must rest while others

watch, I've sorted the whole thing
     out. Four panels, yes?

     A child could do the
algebra: made free, in chains, in

chains, made free. Remorse, which
     you call history, set

     in motion by the paradox.
How many people contribute as

much? My sword, unlike the angel's,
     sheathed, my charge an open

     door. The saint required to
suffer where you see him, extramurally.

5. THE BAPTISM OF THE NEOPHYTES

He knelt because the others knelt. And
          nothing was odd about that except,
unlike the others, he seemed to know

nothing of shame. Which quite astonished
          me. Not brazened-it-out, or
wrapped-himself-in-pridefulness (the surest

sign of struggle), simply free, by what
          conjunction of insight or
ignorance I am still at a loss to imagine,

from the universal misery of fitting-in-
          the-body. We were many
on the hillside, the waters ran shallow

for him as for everyone else, we thought
          this meant nothing to hide.
And it was then I knew the messenger.

For some of us, the treachery's half the
          getting there, we have to be
flayed by our own bad faith. And hence

the scene of washing. You'll remember
          we still thought it had no
limit, that the water and the air it came

from came unendingly, and clean.
          We thought we had fouled
ourselves alone. And then the young one

came and knelt and I could see
          the whole equation, what
we'd gained by it and what we had agreed

to lose. We'd meant to do better by
          those who came after,
that was both the pity and the point.

HER ARGUMENT FOR THE
EXISTENCE OF GOD

This one then: the
doctor, who of course possesses a foreign name, thus
                          gathering all our what
shall we call them our powers of foreboding in a single

sordid corner of
the morning news, contrived to miss the following:
                          eight fractured ribs,
three missing fingertips, infected tissue, torn and partly

healed again,
between the upper lip and gum and, this you have to use
                          your Sunday
finest to imagine, a broken back, third lumbar, which

had all
but severed the spinal cord, leaving him "floppy," or so
                          the coroner later
determined, below the waist. Now granted, she might not have

thought to expect
a wailing one-and-a-half-year-old to toddle obligingly
                          over the tiles nor
felt she had the leisure to apply her little mallet just below the

knee, we see that, but
we are not talking nuance here. The tooth he had swallowed, so
hard had been
the blow to his face—of course one had no inkling, that would

take some sort of
psychic or an MRI. But ulcerated lesions on the scalp and
ears? I tell you if
I hear once more how the underage mother's underage boyfriend

suffered a difficult
childhood himself I'll start to wreck the furniture. When I'm
allowed to run the world you'll
have to get a license just to take the course on parenting and

everyone
will fail it and good riddance we'll die out. But in the
meantime which
is where we're always stranded and ignoring consolation

which is laughable what's
to be made of the sheer bad fit? The reigning brilliance
of the genome and
the risen moon. The cell wall whose electric charge forms now

a channel now

a subtle barrier no modulating thought has thought

                                to equal. The

arachnid's exoskeleton. The kestrel's eye. And we who might

have been worthy but

for reasons forever withheld from us aren't. Wouldn't you

                                rather be damned

for cause?

BLINK

Emil Mayer, Wiener Typen

I don't know what they're called, the chains

                          that seem to be part of the

        harness, but it takes no special powers to see

he won't be getting up again.

The cart piled deep

                        with gunnysacks of lading

        indeterminate, the cobbled

square, the tram rails, all the nascent/ob-

solescent urban tangle of technologies: but

                        something here is

        dying that is not abstract.

He was not rich

who harnessed the horses in leather-and-

                        chains and

        starved them down to gauntness, this is not

the bitter manifest

of one man's hardened heart.
                                        See him now bending
                to disengage
the fallen one from the shaft. So that

the other, the one whose hooves are still
                                        beneath him, neck still
                bearing the weight of the traces through which
he is bound to the one on the

ground, stands quite neglected. It's
                                        Vienna, 1910, the ignorant
                latter days of empire, though
the man with the camera

appears to have comprehended it all. Who loved
                                        above even
                the elbowing crowds at the vegetable stand
the hours with his brush

in the lamplight. First
                                        the visible image bleached
                away, the silvers ever
altered, then

the inking-up, by hand, which resurrects

                         the horses, harness, one

        alarmed and one indifferent passer-by, the

city's open

book of imperturbability.

                            The sufferer? Still

       standing. Neither

passage through brief oblivion nor

the transfer print reversals have done anything

                         to help him. It's

     his job now, he secures the frame.

Ovid in Exile

The Black Sea

Omitting the rust-
bedazzled storage tanks and parched

cement, the cedar-and-pressboard
 pavilion, the border

 of marigolds mustered in
forced good cheer, ignoring

the beachfront disco (closed), the eighteen
 crumbling stations of miniature

golf and now the singer at her microphone
 in solemn Dolly Parton

 aspirational, the bravery's
in the welcome here. The giving-us-more-

than-they've-kept-for-themselves and
 whether we fathom the gift

 or no. The brindled dog
who followed when I walked out on the

pier today observed a formal distance
in the manner of the doomed-

to-starve. Go, little book,
and tell them in the city how I didn't think

to feed her. In the bad years, says the
woman at my table, we managed

to get our hands on oxygen tanks,
but then they mined the river and we had

to give it up. Above the stapled loops
of speaker wire, the spider

has posted her silken advice:
Fear office that forgets itself,

the porter who lets you pass today may
be dismissed tomorrow. Where

a Roman saw plain
nothingness, shut out from all he loved,

the latterday subjects of latterday
empire spent their only lives

shut in. For which
the only cure is living longer than the

tyranny. Now taking the Roman as patron
for love of the word,

they've gathered us here in
festival. Which might have taught the Roman

better manners, had he not been so blinded
by grief. Power's arbitrary

power to strip the hearthstone
of its sustenance. Our ever-renewable

strategies for failing to prevent it. But look:
they've cleared the floor for

dancing. Let's,
our separateness on hold for once, contrive

to show we're grateful.

Varenna

Smothered up in gauze, the sky's
      been healing for a week or

two, conserving its basin of gruel.
      The shops have closed

in sympathy. The ferry's ministrations
      barely mark the hour. And just

when we'd convinced ourselves that
      beauty unsubdued betrays

a coarsened mind, the fabric starts
      to loosen, lift, and daylight

all unblighted takes a gaudy good-
      night bow. What sodden

indistinction just an hour ago had all
      but persuaded us not to

regret resumes its first divisions:
      slate from cinder, ash

from smoke, warm dapple-gray from
    moleskin, dove- from

Quaker-gray from taupe, until
    the blackwater satins unroll their

gorgeous lengths above a sharpening
    partition of lake-and-loam.

Give up yet? says the cirro-strato-sable
    brush. Then watch

what I can do with orange. And,
    flood-lit, ink-besotted, so

assails the upper atmosphere that
    all our better judgment

fails. The Alps? They've seen it all
    before. They've flattened

into waiting mode. The people?
    Flat bedazzled. But

in fairness had a shorter way to fall.

"... More Instructive Than a Long Trip to Europe"

Flannery O'Connor

The wolf, she meant: the lupus.
Which
we also yoke with butterfly:
broad curves across

the cheekbones (finest lesions) and
the narrow bridge
across the nose.
What can I tell you, says

body to soul, to make you understand.
There is
a system, so exquisite in solicitude
for every least

unlocking that sustains you, every atom
scanned
for *friend* or *foe,*
it forms the very script

of self-cohering. In its
zeal sometimes
it goes too far. As if where you'd
always thought home was they

should suddenly take your papers away
and ask you
why you've come here and (no
phone calls) why

you're plotting harm. The body
turns
against itself. And why should it not
be brilliant in this newest

fevered cause as in its every other aptitude?
Salerno,
late twelfth century: Roger Frugard
writes his book. And thinking

wolf bite gives disease a name. No
way of course
to know the inner workings but
he has his Galen, has

his university, medieval on the Roman
                    stones—
            its lovely crenelations grace
                    the painting in my guidebook—

and he has his eyes. A king has come
                    to kneel
            before the surgeons: see
                    his many retainers, the weight

of his robes. Behold the faith we've always
                    placed in
            learning. And the feral counter-
                    argument, encoded in the blood.

STILL LIFE

I

His ears his mouth his
    nostrils having filled

    with ash, his cheekbones
chin (all ash) and on the ash a tide

of seawrack that cannot
    be right a trail of scum or

    vomit then and either
his shoulder's been crushed by the

blast or angled on the stretcher so
    oddly that raising

    his arm to ward us off
he seems to be more damaged than he

is, and eyes
    that should have cracked the

    camera. This was not
the current nightmare this was two

or three nightmares ago, the men
were loading plums and

peaches onto trucks at
Qaa. And though in my lucky and

ignorant life I have never so much as
encountered the scent

of explosives (I
had taken a different bus that day,

the city I live in is thicker with
doctors than all of Beka'a

is thick with bombs), I've
seen those eyes before exactly.

Failures of decency closer to home.

2

(The clearing of the ghetto)

Red wool, and falsely brightened, since
we need the help.

A child because
the chambers of the heart will hold so

little. If the filmmaker, having
apprenticed in fables,

proposes a scale for which,
he hopes, we're apt and if

this bigger-than-a-breadbox slightly-
smaller-than-the-microwave is

just about the vista we can
manage, let's agree to call it history, let's

imagine we had somehow seen its face
in time. But where

in all of Kraków is
the mother who buttoned her coat?

A city steeped in harm-to-come,
the film stock drained

to gray. The sturdy
threading-forward of a child who

might be panicked by the crowd but
                    has her mind now on

a hiding place. Our
childlike conviction that she shall be

spared. Mistake that brings
                    the lesson home: we lack

                    retention.
Chalk mark on a clouded screen.

                    3

But what was it like, his dying?
                    It was like

                    a distillation.
You had morphine? We had

morphine, but he couldn't use
                    the bed. *The bed?*

                    His lungs were so
thickened with tumors and phlegm

he had no way of breathing there.
                    You'd rented the bed?

beside it

hen something

had

y with him.

m in his

we thought

to

e

s

y-

ave-me-alone,

ur-sense-

will

die myself.

eaning well

nough.

ant that he

this wasn't lost on us.

The urn that h

    a better

4

Sister partrid

    The

    wi

have read

the bount

    and

    that br

the leisure that

I have come to thi

    the argume

    a simpler poi

for example, where th

the pores, the pith, the l

    heart of it, each d

    boundary bound to

Meaning death, of course, th

He climbed down
and asked for his tools. W

was broken he fixed it, that
always been the wa

So then . . . We left h
chair. But as the day went on

he needed bedding so we tried
lift him. That's the on

he blamed us. *That'*
the look you meant. The wh

can't-you-people-just-le
the where-is-yo

of-shame. I
remember it until I

You meant well. M
was not e

We me
should know

olds his ashes does

job.

ge, brother hare.
linen on the table

th its hemstitch. I
the books on pridefulness:

of game park and sideboard
loom, the ships

ought the lemon trees,
masters the view. But

nk
nt-by-likeness makes

nt. The lemon,
e knife has been:

uminescent
ifferential

open.
e un-

protected flesh about to turn, but just
		before the turn, while looking

		can still be an act of praise.
I see you in the mirror every morning

where you wait for me. The linen,
		Father, lemon, knife,

		the pewter with its lovely
reluctance to shine. As though

the given world had given us
		a second chance.

Slaters' Measure

I was fourteen: BBC interview with Collyweston slater David Ellis, 2007.
Bedding plane, quarry sap, etc.: www.stoneroof.org.uk and links. On nineteenth-
century slate mining: J. W. Judd, *The Geology of Rutland and Parts of Lincoln,
Leicester, Huntingdon and Cambridge,* Memoir of the Geological Survey, London,
HMSO, 1875, and Simon Winchester, *The Map That Changed the World: William
Smith and the Birth of Modern Geology,* HarperCollins, 2001.

Lately, I've taken to

Forty percent: Unfortunately, what the speaker heard was correct. NASA studies
confirm an unprecedented forty percent loss in the ozone layer above the north-
ern Arctic in the winter of 2010–11.

Getting and Spending

Isabella Whitney: the first woman in England to write poetry for commercial
publication; her books appeared in 1567 and 1573.

Ariadne in Triumph

Accounts of Ariadne's abandonment by Theseus on the island of Naxos are
wildly inconsistent, but one major tradition has her later becoming consort to
Dionysus/Bacchus. Roman sarcophagus: the "Bacchus Sarcophagus," Kelsey
Museum of Archaeology, Ann Arbor, Michigan. This poem is dedicated to
Thomas Lynch.

Theseus Forgetting

Your children against the rocks: Theseus' son Hippolytus was dragged to death
by his own horses. Theseus was to blame and lived to know it.

Dido Refuses to Speak

The child: In Marlowe's version of the story, Cupid assumes the guise of Ascanius, son of Aeneas, and touches Dido's breast with his golden arrow. The oxhide: For this account, see Marcus Junianus Justinus, *Epitome of the Philippic History of Pompeius Trogus,* Book XVIII. "Dido Refuses to Speak" was originally written as part of a commission for composer Susan Botti and the Blakemore Trio and premiered, as section 3 of *The Gates of Silence,* in Nashville and New York, February/March 2010. The sequence is dedicated to Susan Botti.

From the Life of Saint Peter

His Shadow: Acts 5:15. The Death of Ananias: Acts 5:1–10. The Tribute Money: Matthew 17:24–27. The Expulsion / Saint Peter Released from Prison: Genesis 3:22–24 / Acts 12:6–10. The Baptism of the Neophytes: Acts 2:37–41.

Blink

Emil Mayer (1871–1938). For details on the biography and on the bromoil photographic process, see Edward Rosser's essay in *Viennese Types [Wiener Typen],* Blind River Editions, 1999.

Ovid in Exile

For Liliana Ursu.

Still Life

Section 2: *Schindler's List,* dir. Steven Spielberg, 1993.